CH(

WISDOM

MARK BRANDON READ

CHOPPER'S WISDOM

JOHN BLAKE

Published by John Blake Publishing Ltd,
3, Bramber Court, 2 Bramber Road,
London W14 9PB, England

www.blake.co.uk

First published in paperback in 2005

ISBN 1 84454 183 5

British Library Cataloguing-in-Publication Data:

A catalogue record for this book is available from the British Library.

Design by www.envydesign.co.uk

Printed and bound in Great Britain by William Clowes Ltd, Beccles, Suffolk

1 3 5 7 9 10 8 6 4 2

Papers used by John Blake Publishing are natural, recyclable products
made from wood grown in sustainable forests. The manufacturing processes
conform to the environmental regulations of the country of origin.

Every attempt has been made to contact the relevant copyright-holders,
but some were unobtainable. We would be grateful if the appropriate people
could contact us.

Mark Brandon 'Chopper' Read is everyone's favourite criminal. His witty memoirs have kept readers enthralled for years and no matter what the subject, Chopper has something to say. From death and murder to pregnancy and underwear shopping, Chopper can't fail to make you laugh. So we decided it was about time we gave you this – a handy little book filled with his best phrases, pearls of wisdom and general 'chopperisms'.

 Enjoy!

CHOPPER ON ...
THE ART OF VIOLENCE AND THE LIFE OF CRIME

'**A** general bit of shooting makes you forget your troubles and take the mind off the cost of living.'

'**Men who are forced to kill or be killed in the criminal world are another story, as what they do isn't real murder. It is simply the way it is and the way it has to go … kill or be killed is not murder in my book.**'

'Most escape plots are hatched out of boredom. Prisoners want something to keep them interested. When you have people spending all their waking hours thinking about something they end up finding an answer. That is why there is no such thing as an escape-proof jail. If the human mind is capable of designing and building it, the human mind is capable of beating it.'

'CurlyBill once rode 300 miles to kill three men in the Red Dog Saloon. I myself would have taken a taxi. Which brings me to a matter of financial concern. If you were a professional killer, could you write off cab fares like that as a tax deduction?

Surely a hit man could claim, guns, bullets and such like as business expenses. It seems only fair.'

'When the man from the city robs you he will do it with a gun to your head or a blade at your throat and have the manners to wear a mask, whereas the man from the bush will do it with a firm handshake and a warm smile.'

'It seems to me that terrorism is a weapon of anger and not of intelligence.'

'I know I talk about guns a lot, but I get pleasure from them. They are my tools of trade, but they are also my hobby. I must confess, although it is not much of a secret, that I do enjoy shooting a total arsewipe.'

'To me it is a game and if you are caught, then it is no use howling and pretending that you are some whiter than white saint who has never done the wrong thing. Many crims eventually convince themselves that they didn't do it, even when they are caught with the smoking gun in their hands and there are 100 witnesses prepared to swear that they saw the bloke pull the trigger.

I am not like that. If I did it and I am caught, then it's a fair cop and you do the time without complaining.'

'The average crook involved in these criminal war situations has no flair or imagination. If they are prepared to listen and follow my advice I'll help.

11

I love a good criminal war or battle situation and I am only ever consulted on matters of violence and death.'

'But in the true world of criminal "bang bang you're dead" violence it doesn't matter how well you can fight, or play footy. If your number comes up you are off tap and that is that. Dead as a bloody mackerel, no questions asked.'

'I mean, getting stabbed, shot, bashed, verballed, slandered, abused, betrayed while being investigated by your own side while upholding law and order and the good of the community … this is meant to be a career?'

'You can't complain that you only pulled your weapon out to frighten the policeman and that you weren't really going to use it. If you pull a weapon out on someone to scare them, then you stand a bloody good chance of scaring them into blowing your bloody head off.

Silly bastards. The more crims and nutters who get blown away by police and the more police who get blown away by the crims and nutters, the more paranoid and frightened both sides become.

So welcome to America. It's what Australia wanted, to copy America. But whereas cats have nine lives, copy cats get only one.'

'All this needless violence is caused by too much television, if you ask me. Bloody Aussie land is going mad, and in my opinion the whole bloomin' country could do with a valium, a good cup of tea and a nice lie down.'

'My enemies have fallen, weakened and run because they have placed more importance on their own lives than I did. Don't misunderstand, I don't want to die. I want to live as long as God allows. But I don't fear death. As long as my death has a certain amount of style, flair and dash involved, I don't mind.'

'I will never surrender. I will fight on in the face of unbeatable odds. I simply will not plead guilty to a crime that I simply did not do. Why should I? Would you? I think not. So why should I be forced to plead guilty on a matter I didn't do just because I am a career criminal.'

'Once the blood starts flying, politics and talk won't solve anything.'

'I have grown to despise and loathe the mainstream criminal population, for they are nothing but weak-gutted mice.'

'If you get to the frontline of a war you can be the safest.'

'Now the crims are feeding off each other. They have become cannibals. The dope dealers are all robbing each other, the bank robbers are robbing each other, the massage parlours are standing over each other, the night club owners are standing over and robbing each other.'

'If people want fair play, let them join a cricket club. A street fight is a no-holds-barred, anything-goes battle between two men or ten men. Anything can be used, from a slap on the face with a wet tea towel to a meat axe through the

brain. Mainly fists, feet, knees and head butts are used, if a heavy object is not close to hand.'

'But guts without guns in my world can be fatal.'

'It now appears to me that I can only trust someone when I have a loaded gun stuck in their mouth.'

'One thing I want to make very clear as a criminal, I am in a class that is no threat whatsoever to Mr and Mrs Average. The normal honest person has nothing to fear from me. Chopper Read won't break into your home, he won't pinch your TV, video or purse. He won't rape your daughter, wife, sister or granny. He won't pinch your car, rob your bank, café or off-licence.

No, I am not in an area of crime which would personally touch the lives of the ordinary individual. I am not even in an area of crime that will touch the ordinary criminal. I am, or was, in a league alone, working in a specialised area of crime that the ordinary type of criminal only comes into contact with in his nightmares.'

'I know my not guilty plea is a fart in the face of a thunderstorm.'

'I don't take wounded men to hospital. I don't even take dead men to the morgue.'

'He looked quite surprised when I pulled out my trusty meat cleaver and slammed it down on the bar, removing his four fingers at the knuckle.'

'To me violence was an art, and I was the artist.'

'A nice bit of sharp pain clears the mind and cleanses the soul. I personally see the lash as a bloody good character builder. If you can't hang them, lash them and if you can't lash them, bash them.'

'The criminal world is populated by three basic types – social spastics, mental retards and brain-dead junkies. There is also a smattering of freaks and flukes.

If you are a social spastic, a mental retard or a brain-dead junkie, or even a freak, and you haven't been caught or jailed, then you are definitely a fluke.'

'In Australia it is considered perfectly wonderful to talk at length about what you would like to do, and providing you never do it no man will raise his voice against you. But if you get off your arse and get out there and actually do it the critics will knock you.

Criminals are told to pick themselves up, dust themselves off, and improve themselves.

But the very, very few who have tried to do just that are widely condemned.'

'Criminals are told to mend their ways and improve themselves, but when we do, the rules get changed. The people who run the game not only have the umpires in their pocket, but they move the bloody goal posts half way through the match. How can you win?'

'Death never brawls in the street. Death never has to throw a punch. Death only smiles, puts his hand inside his coat and says in a quiet voice, "Excuse me, mate, I didn't quite hear that. Were you talking to me?"

Men found blown away in car parks have generally been stupid enough to invite death outside for a fist fight.

Death never has to raise his voice or his fist in anger, the most polite and well-mannered gent you will ever meet in the world is the hangman.'

'Lesson: don't ever question the impact of a gun at a criminal arms deal. Not unless you have tin legs, anyway.'

'I will never surrender my guns.'

'The professional policeman and the professional criminal: there is not a lot to separate them.'

The Shifty Deal

The Australian Courts don't hold no grudge,
A nod's as good as a wink,
To a blind Judge,
No need for cash, the brief's been paid,
All praise the name of Legal Aid,
The Crown is hoping for an early night,
No need to struggle,
No need to fight,
"Look, boys, I'll drop this,
You plead to that."
And all home in time,
To feed the cat,

No cash needed here,
Nor money down,
Forget the Yanks,
This is Melbourne Town,
"I'll do this for you,
You do that for me,
We can sort this out,
Just wait and see,"
The courts, crooks and coppers all know the feel,
Of the classic Aussie shifty deal.

CHOPPER ON ...
WOMEN

'There are women banging on the gates trying to get in to visit me, others ringing the prison crying over the phone pleading to talk to me, and others writing me pornographic love letters. But when I am on the outside, things change. If I was standing in a room full of nympho-maniacs, I could swing a cat and not hit a soul.'

'A pair of long legs can walk through doors otherwise closed. A set of big tits and a pair of big eyes and an even bigger smile can float through the valley of the shadow of death like a butterfly.'

'The chick could talk the leg off an elephant and probably deep throat one as well, from the look of her. She had a mouth wider than Mich Jagger's. As a married man I am no longer meant to notice these things, but as an author I am allowed to. It's called literary licence, and it's a lot easier to get than a gun licence. So you can all get stuffed.'

'Don't ever go shopping with your wife. I needed some new underpants. I'm now tipping the

scales at a dainty eighteen stone. I waited outside the store trying to act debonair and Mary-Ann selected several pairs of extra extra large jockey-type underpants.

The sales girl and her various sales-lady friends gathered as well as lady shoppers and held the offending garments up for inspection. Other ladies came over and inspected the underwear then Mary-Ann called me over. I had to walk through a small army of smiling girls, mothers, shoppers and sales ladies while the jumbo mansize lingerie was held up against my embarrassed person for further inspection. Ladies, girls, onlookers came from everywhere. Chopper Read was buying underpants. This was a must-see moment ... "I just want a couple of sets of underpants," I said. "Big ones." I was so embarrassed I would have bought anything to get out of there.

I turned and walked out, waiting in the street outside. Mary-Ann followed along having purchased two pairs of jumbo jockey shorts that could have doubled as circus tents. '"Don't take me shopping with you again," I said. "In future just get me big underpants, socks and T-shirts."

I could not believe what she had just put me through. And I thought prison was bad.'

'Female lawyers can have a great bedside manner but are prone to losing cases. Never allow the charms of a lady lawyer to sway you from common sense.'

'Let's just say I knew of one lady lawyer who wore stockings and a suspender belt, stiletto high heels and the works under her black dress and robe and would allow a certain client to run his hand up her leg in the Supreme Court interview room ... When a guy is locked up in prison the mind can play tricks.

When a lady lawyer pops into the prison on a Sunday wearing runners and a baggy tracksuit and the poor prisoner is called up to the professional visit area to see his lawyer and the tracksuit pants come down and she invites the client to hump the arse off her it tends to soften the word guilty.'

'Of the several hundred love letters I have got in jail, I have developed a good filing system. You may remember that while in jail I have to go without a private secretary. The letters from old, ugly or fat chicks go in the bin. Cruel, you may think. Well, put it this way, if you are silly enough to write a love letter with a photo included to a self-confessed arsehole, then you better make sure you are good looking, or it's straight into the old round filing cabinet.'

'If you want to know about a bloke then talk to the chick who's got him by the dick.'

'The point is that my feelings towards women are the same as my feelings towards men. I've met some fantastic ones and I've found some diamonds in my life, but in general they are a steaming great shower of shit that I wouldn't piss on. As a rule, if the female of the species did not provide a sexual advantage, the male of the species wouldn't even engage the buggers in conversation.

Call me old-fashioned.'

'One lady ended up in tears after proudly showing me her brand-new boob-enlargement job. Most impressive. I advised her to go back and get her face fixed as a job lot. Ha, ha. Who said stand-up is dead?'

'Mary-Ann is going to have a baby. I told her that we will have to go to the doctor and find out what caused it, then we must stop doing it right away.'

'Walking is good exercise, and I need it. Walking the dog beats spanking the monkey any day.

Most men my age would be happy to walk Miss Nude Australia across the paddocks with a dog or two, giving new meaning to the words "watch those puppies bounce". We had two puppies, a fine pussy and half a mongrel all out in the fresh air.'

'After a lifetime of study, I have come up with what I believe to be a rock solid doctrine on the vexing topic of female of the species, and it would be selfish of me not to share it.

I see all females without exception as suffering from a mental and emotional psychosis that I call "the schizophrenic condition". It isn't their fault; it's just the way it is. They tend to be insecure, afraid, puzzled, confused, worried, concerned, ill at ease and lacking self esteem and self-confidence. Not only that, they are dizzy, scatty, flighty, totally withdrawn from reality and tend to totally distort of reality. And loving, hateful, possessive, jealous, greedy, generous, dreamers and fantasy merchants living in a world of romantic imagination … they have a list of mental and emotional disorders a mile long all on the boil. Add the sex and the motherhood urge to this and you have a totally neurotic, obsessional, anxious, head banging, raving, ranting nut case of the highest and most dangerous order.

In other words the classic schizophrenic condition. We are talking about human beings who undergo twelve separate mood swings every twelve hours.'

'I have pulled all the pictures of girls from my walls. I have become sick and tired of prison staff and other inmates perving on pictures of some of my good friends who happen to be female ... I have decided to get rid of them because with some of the comments made about them I would end up pulling some

bastard's eye out, which would not look good when I am trying to convince the High Court that I am the male version of Mother Teresa. So I have put up pictures of the Derwent Valley in their place. It has helped calm everyone down, me included. I have never had a dream of covering the Derwent Valley with whipped cream and then licking it off.'

'Falling in lust with them [prostitutes] was fine but falling in love was foolish, and that should you be unlucky enough to fall in love with a cracker then stab yourself in the back because if you don't then little Miss Tragic Magic will do it for you … It is hard to trust a girl who loves everyone and kisses each man's heart with a different lie on her lips. My problem is that in my youth I had the misfortune to fall under the spell of several ladies of the night and found myself betrayed.'

'It's quite amazing. Here I sit with a no-eared toothless head that even a mother wouldn't love and I've got the screws of Risdon shooing the sheilas away with a stick. God's idea of a practical joke? I can't figure it out.'

'Women understand sex, but they do not understand the psychology of fear. For women the answer is simple. Understand what is happening to you and if you don't like it, smile, play along nicely and stab the bastard in the back at the first opportunity. Ha. Ha.'

Lady Killer

I never killed a lady, and I really don't know why,
Most of the ones I've met have really
deserved to die,
I guess in the end,
In spite of my mind being bent,
I'm just a bloody old softy,
A real old-fashioned gent.

CHOPPER ON ...
Being an Author

'While some may think the pen is mightier than the sword, let me say that I will give up my gun when they pry it from my cold dead fingers.'

'I have written a book and people seem to think I walk about all day in a smoking jacket stuffed full of cash and live on champagne and caviar. In fact, people think I have become a millionaire through writing. Let me tell you I made more money with a blow torch than a ball point. And I didn't get too much out of the crime world either.'

'There is the elite class – killer poets like my good self who can write, fight, bite, light, smite and, when need be, say goodnight.'

'While I was inside I got mail by the truck load. Much of it is nice but some is rather puzzling. I have heard from literary critics and lounge chair intellectuals telling me that my books have no real message. Well, first of all, the only literary critic I really care about is the cash register, and when it stops ringing I will know I have hit a false note.

As far as intellectuals are concerned, an intellectual is someone who spends all his time giving other people the answers to questions he didn't understand in the first place. They go

through life dreaming up new ways to fix problems that they themselves created.'

'When I write the truth I am faced with verbal bullets from my critics and real ones from my enemies. Words are like magic stardust to be thrown into the eyes of men to confuse and inform at the same time.

The pen is mightier than the sword but in fairness to the sword great things have been done by men and swords. But without the pen the actions of the sword would not be remembered beyond one generation.'

'She [Mary-Ann] once called me away from my writing to come and see the way Poop Foot our cat was sitting. Do all great writers have to put up with this? No wonder Hemingway topped himself. At least he had a double barrelled shotgun to do it with.'

'Fact is stranger than fiction – sometimes so strange that it is downright hard to believe – they shout and laugh at reality, Or maybe truth is a bit humdrum and ordinary for them. The fiction writer can turn a bullet in the guts into an epic thriller, whereas in reality a slug in the guts is not worth more than a page.

An act of violence, whether broken glass in the neck, or a bullet in a body, is over in the blink of an eye, and to write about it should not take more than a page or so. That is why I will never be accepted as a proper writer by other writers. I tell it how it is … bang, bang, no bullshit, then on to the next story. I have been there, I have done it and for mine you cannot turn a ten-second stabbing into a ten chapter epic. Not unless you are a fiction writer that is. And I'm a fighter, not a writer. I know about verbals not verbs. Guns, not grammar.'

'If the authorities tried to stop some government-subsidised, black tee-shirt wearing academic trendy, of questionable sexuality, from writing some boring 60-page book about the mating habits of Tibetan yaks, the civil libertarians would be protesting in the streets.

But because the author is a Good Ol' Boy with

no ears, who is popular with the book-buying public, and therefore not seen as trendy, then no-one has lifted a finger.'

'The truth is that all I ever wanted to do was write a cook book. I was going to call it: "How to Kill Them in the Kitchen".'

'I don't know what it is about ladies and guns, but there is a definite psychological effect when you mix the two. They get an excited gleam in their eyes and just blast away as if there is no tomorrow.'

'Pregnant women are a beautiful things, but you could get whiplash trying to keep up with the mood swings.

Sadly, when she should be concentrating on sleeping and getting bigger with our unborn son she decides to become a part-time literary critic.'

CHOPPER ON ...
CHOPPER

'What I lack in the finer points of fisticuffs I make up for in violence.'

'You don't get a reputation like mine for being a nice guy.'

'Why is it that every time I wave at a psychiatrist from a distance of 300 metres he tosses a handful of pills down my neck? … The have just given me my nightly "bomb me out pill" and the white clouds are rolling in.'

'Chopper Read has left the stage and is just sitting in a chicken shed playing cards with Elvis. No guns allowed.'

'Have seen so much pain and suffering in my life. I have had people die in my arms and die at my hand. I thought I could not sink any lower but I was wrong. I have now been lowered into the abyss of Hell.

I have been banned from the only pub in town.'

'Then again, what would I know?? I'm just a roaring drunk, a hopeless liar or a roaring liar and a hopeless drunk, or so some would have you believe.'

'I didn't get these scars in a fight over the sushi tray at a crime writers' conference, and the claw hammer hole in my head didn't come from a dispute with the scone lady over the strawberry jam.'

'Why did I have my ears chopped off? ... I told them, "I will be leaving H Division, tomorrow." They said, "No, you won't," and I said I would. So I went back and got Kevin to cut my bloody ears off. You reckon I didn't leave H Division straight away? The classo board nearly came down and carried me out themselves.

The first time it happened it was big news, then everyone started doing it, nothing to do with me. Then all the nutcases in here thought there was something to be gained out of this. I was the president of the Van Gogh club until Garry David cut his penis off. I wrote to him, "You can take over." When the dicky birds start hitting the pavement I thought it was time to resign.

Enduring a bit of pain is one thing, but that's a bit much.'

'I always feel uncomfortable when anyone asks me for my autograph. I'm not a rock star; I'm a crook who wrote a book, and the psychology of wanting an autograph from me is wanting it for its novelty freak value.'

'Now, if they had a "shoot a drug-dealer in the eye competition", I am sure I would win the gold.'

'Kill me or cop it sweet, that's the way I saw it. In or out of prison no one could take more pain than me, no one could dish out more pain than me. I wasn't about to stand in the shadow of any man who went before me.'

'I'm already punch drunk in charge of limited intelligence as it is.'

'Ahh, Chopper, you old trend setter. But as I said to the boys, if you really want to look like the Chopper, get them bloody ears off. The mention of a razor blade slicing through the ears soon separates the men from the boys.'

'I swallowed my own top teeth myself years ago. They bloody nearly killed me going down and it was an uncomfortable experience getting them out the other end.

So the message to all you kiddies is, brush after meals so that you don't end up with false teeth. Because if you do, it can hurt both ends.'

'I am without a shadow of a doubt the fastest eater in captivity, bar maybe the odd polar bear in a zoo somewhere.'

'I can shovel down steak, eggs, sausages, mushrooms and mixed veggies and sweets in under three minutes with total propriety. I have perfect manners. I eat like Prince Charles would if he was on Angel Dust.'

'G Division ... was the area kept in jail for the mentally unwell. I had obviously been put there by mistake, ha ha. I was actually sent there after I mislaid my ears. Obviously, those in power thought this was not the act of a well unit.'

'I am confident that I hold the bashing record inside Pentridge ... and it will never be beaten.'

'There is no evidence of psychiatric disorder in Mr. Read. He clearly has a most unusual personality, but then, that would be expected of someone who is not uncomfortable about being regarded as a professional criminal.'

Taken from a psychiatric report
on Mark Brandon Read.

'Just because a man has a few tattoos, a criminal record and a love of blood doesn't make him a hard man.'

'If anyone farts in my general direction, from a distance of 300 yards, they are in bother. Ha ha.'

'I was leading the mentally ill, but in my own way I was the worst of them all. I had the smiling face of a young angel, and a heart so full of tears that there was no room for the blood to flow. I was emotionally and mentally twisted. As a young guy I was cruel, cold and totally without human mercy, feeling or compassion.

I didn't feel hate. I was just emotionally numb. All I had was my own sense of right and wrong. I saw everything only in terms of battles and strategies. I lived to spill the blood of enemies, and there were plenty of them.

I am almost gentle and overflowing with

**human kindness when I look at myself now,
compared with what I was.'**

'Let's face it, I was as nutty as a fruit cake. Thank God, I'm all better now.

Ha, ha, ha.'

**'I see myself as the typical Aussie male.
Sure I may be covered in tattoos, have no ears,
have a criminal record you can't jump over and
torture drug dealers for profit and pleasure,
but I personally see those as minor
cosmetic differences.**

**Underneath it all, I am just like the next
bloke. I like a laugh, a drink, shooting**

scumbags and, most of all, when I am on the outside, I like a bet.'

'If people don't like me they can either kill me or cop it sweet, and until I am in my grave they can stick it as far as I'm concerned. To hell with them all.

Their hatred is like sunshine to me. I thrive on it. There is something about me that seems to inflame hatred and passion in many people. I just don't understand it myself. To me I am just your everyday normal killer, but to others I seem to be the devil in disguise.'

'I am like a magnet to the mentally ill.'

'The truth is that I will never make enough money to buy anything for anybody. I have a team of lawyers to support. After all, charity begins at home.'

'My reputation in the criminal world has always been based on other people's hatred, fear and paranoia. My image has been made by my enemies, whereas a host of big-name crooks have reputations which come from their friends, admirers and hangers-on.'

'I fell out with Dennis Allen the way I have fallen out with most people … I belted him.'

'He used to talk so much about all the violence it went in one ear and out the other. Or so to speak ... I don't have any ears.'

'Those who know me well will tell you I love a bit of a debate, although they might also say I like to finish the discussion with a baseball bat or a blow torch. I have found in the past that lethal weapons tend to get opponents to see the logic of your argument.'

'Maybe it's some sort of midlife crisis. Once I used to think I was immortal; now it's suddenly hit me that I'm not. Bloody hell. It's a shock when you approach forty and find yourself sitting in a prison cell, realising you have spent nearly twenty of those forty years behind bars. What a waste.

Even as a kid I was always a bit of a backyard philosopher. In those days I always believed that the cornerstone of all correct thinking was that good will conquer evil. But as you get older you learn that evil built the world, and when the so-called great and good men of history wished to achieve great and good things, they did not hesitate to walk over the bodies of millions of people to achieve their ends.

So what is good and what is evil? It's all a psychological blur. When a private individual kills a few people, he or she is a monster. But when a politician kills a few million he goes down in history as a man of great vision.'

'I personally wouldn't have the bad manners to put anybody in a boot – alive that is. It'd be far too uncomfortable for that.'

'There is not a gunman alive who frightens me, but I became terrified of people in shops, especially of fat ladies in lambs' wool slippers. They would scream out, "Look, that's the bloke on the telly. He's a murderer."

Call me sensitive, but I couldn't cop that.'

'I would relieve any man of his heart and lungs with a double barrel shotgun if he tried to turn his hand against me or mine. In other words, hurt me or mine and I'll cut your ears off, put a hole in your

manners and I'll rip your bloody nose off with a
pair of multi-grips.'

**'Not many people will believe this, particularly
those that I have bashed, or had their feet
warmed with the gas blowtorch, but I don't feel
hate. I just don't know what it feels like. I mean,
I can pretend to hate, but the most I can feel is
to be a little cross with someone.'**

'My attitude was that if you don't carry your gun on
you, you might as well not have a gun at all.'

'I go out of my way to avoid three things: manual labour, physical exercise and fisticuffs.'

'I do all my fighting with a gun in one hand and a cup of tea in the other. While the world is full of people who could bash me, the world is not full of people who could bash me and live to talk about it. That's why God invented razor blades, butcher's knives, iron bars, meat axes and guns that go bang – so blokes like me don't get bashed 10 times a day before breakfast.

If people want to try and bash me that's fine, as long as they don't mind spending the rest of their lives in a wheelchair or being led around by a seeing-eye dog.

If they really want to rock and roll, then it would be

a coffin for them. The only thing I get bashed with these days is bullshit. Shoot me, but for goodness sake, don't shit me, as the old saying goes.'

'I get mail from some people who see me as some sort of Robin Hood, a crusader who has set himself up to clean the world of drug dealers ... I don't want people to get the wrong impression. I don't take from the rich and give to the poor. I keep the money myself. My life will never be made into a Disney movie. It is business. It is not and has never been some sort of holy crusade. But it can be fun, and quite profitable too.'

'When I look back on the jelly beans I have shot, stabbed, bashed, iron-barred, axed, knee-capped, toe-cut, blow-torched, killed and generally up-ended, I look at it like this: if I hadn't done it, then somebody else would have. I am not the only lion in the jungle, but I am the only one with no ears and a smiling face.'

CHOPPER ON ...
PRISON

'Some prisoners like to waffle on about the dark and lonely solitude of their damp and lonely cell and how they forgot the sound of the cell door slamming for the first time. What a load of crap. One cell is the same as any other. When you have heard one cell door slam you have heard them all. Jail life can be summed up in two words: petty and boring.'

'After the years that I have done inside I would write 1,000 pages on jail life. But men who have done it, lived it, bled it, cried and nearly died in it, couldn't be bothered.

I'll leave that all to one-month wonders, who can write a gripping thriller based on their blood-chilling adventures in Her Majesty's Motel.'

Sanity in Cell 37

In a world feeding on war and fear,
A world starving of love,
I watched a man drowning in blood and the tears,
Of a sick and dying dove,
A total enigma, a puzzle misunderstood,
Seen as evil in his attempts to do good,
They paid him in torment and emotional pain,
For trying to save us from nuclear rain,
And why, I asked, does he even care,
For a world that cares nothing for him,
Apathy, he answered, that's our greatest sin,

He spoke of a nuclear nightmare that will come
upon us all,
It's just a question of time before our Rome will fall,
I read a bit about him and what he was meant to be,
Some said he was CIA, some said he was KGB,
The answer's there, the answer's clear,
But still they fail to see,
He screams words of sanity to the def, dumb
and blind,
So they locked him away with the criminally ill,
But he's not one of our kind, nor if he a dill,
I see a rage within him others fail to see,
In his utter frustration and the knowledge he can't
prevent what he knows he will be,
The anti-nuclear warrior, or the monster from
Death Heaven,
The nightmare prophet in cell 37.

CHOPPER ON ...
FRIENDSHIP

'I had a deep sense of friendship, but over the years the more knives that got stuck in my back and the more times I was betrayed, that sense of friendship becomes less and less.'

'To be stabbed by the same bloke that I tried to get out of jail is a terrible lesson, a good lesson, but a hard way to learn.'

'Chopper's golden rule is that when the shit hits the fan, keep an eye on the people closest to you. The graveyards are full of blokes who got put there by their friends.'

'Friendship is a funny thing. When the good times roll everyone wants to rock and roll with you and when the shit hits the fan you're on your own.'

'The enemy of my enemy is my friend.'

'He was told that I was out to kill him and I was told that he was going to kill me. We both felt that our first meeting would be in the streets

with guns blazing ... Now that we are friends, the only thing we fight about is when he puts too much garlic in our lunchtime curry.'

'Nothing that happens these days seems the same as it once was, and while I live in the present I constantly miss the dead friends of old. All my life people have been coming into my life leaving their mark on my mind, heart and soul, and then dying on me or vanishing into the mists of time. It makes me sad and sentimental.'

The Jew

He wants no glory, he wants no fame,
Very few men have heard his name.
But as a hunter, he's the best I know
Non-stop dash, non-stop go,
He sets to work, without a care,
The smell of burning flesh in the air,
He loves to hunt the big deal prankster,
The nightclub flashy ganster,
He plants them in the ground,
Never to be seen,
Safe and sound,
And before they die, they sometimes ask,
Please tell me who are you,
And with a toothless grin, he looks down
and says,
Just call me Dave the Jew.

CHOPPER ON ...
DRUG DEALERS

'I find the selling of drugs to be a girlish, limp-wristed way to earn one's living. It is the wimp's way to gain wealth and power. Why should I steal drugs when I can simply rob the drug seller?'

'There are two main reasons why I target drug dealers. First, they are the ones with the big money. One is hardly going to make a big profit from kidnapping and torturing men who pinch washing machines for a living, so it's simply a matter of logical economics.'

CHOPPER ON ...
FEAR

'An enemy can cripple itself with its own fear.'

'Everyone fears the unknown; everyone gets a jump in their hearts out of a bump in the night. Everybody wants to go to heaven but nobody wants to die first.'

'Then, through the use of personal contact via the telephone or even a nice card or flowers you can turn up the heat. Bumping into their old mother with a warm smile and a hello, and asking her to pass on your regards to Sonny Boy. Paranoia and fear combine to create an almost crippled mental state. The war at that stage has been won, and I haven't left my lounge chair.

The actual physical part of this form of combat via a death or act of violence is a small part. It is the very last move on the chess board. I play this game over a period of time to create the maximum tension and stress.'

'As a wise man once said, "Kill one, scare one thousand." Even the strong and strong-minded can fall victim, as they can't realise it is happening to them. They can't separate the mind game from the reality. The Psychology of Fear.'

'Using fear correctly is a skill, even an art. Its correct use, I believe, is to instil fear in your targets with a wink and a smile – using courtesy and a friendly, polite attitude … After all, as our mothers taught us, a spoonful of sugar helps the medicine go down.'

'I have outlined the theory before that lust attacks the groin first, the brain second and then the heart. Love attacks the heart first, the brain second and then the groin. Fear attacks only the brain, then cripples every other part of the body.'

'Love, lust and hate are the basic emotions and feelings that the average person deals with. Fear is not something the average person has to confront or even wishes to confront in an average lifetime. So using fear and controlling it is not something that the average person has to do The basic fear that sits in all men's hearts is that each man knows himself. Despite the opinions of others, every man is aware that deep down he is not as good as others think, and that, one day, that may be exposed.'

'Fear is a phantom, a puff of smoke that can be blown into the eyes to cloud the mind and thoughts. It can destroy logic and reason if you do not understand it. How true is the saying, "We have nothing to fear but fear itself".'

CHOPPER ON ...
LIFE AFTER CRIME

'All I can do is put my best foot forward. But if, now and again, I put my best foot on the thick neck of some smartarse, that is not returning to crime, for God's sake.

But just because the lion has left the jungle, it doesn't mean that he automatically turns into a monkey. I am what I am and I am who I am and I cannot and will not change my mental and emotional makeup. Walking away hasn't meant that I have gone through a personality reconstruction.'

'The screws joke with me about marrying into the landed gentry when they see the Jag-driving farmer's daughter come to visit. Ha ha.

Grave digger I may be, but gold digger? Never. Mary-Ann has no brothers and only one sister and there were various crude jests about Mr Hodge not losing a daughter but gaining a Chopper, and at least I'd have plenty of room down on the farm to bury the bodies. (Memo to all authorities and potential in-laws ... the bodies bit was a joke).'

'As with old football players, boxers and sportsmen, in any physical high-risk area there comes a time to walk away. The ones who end up dead are mostly men who over-stayed their time. When the barman yells last orders you leave, and I left.

Had I stayed on I would have become more a figure of comedy than a figure of fear. There is nothing more embarrassing in my opinion than some over-the-hill old fart who still thinks he's a tough guy.'

'It's like a dog on a chain. You put the dog on the chain for the night then let him off the chain in the morning and he runs around and around the back yard like a raving nutter.

You lock a man in a cage for a year or two or longer, then let him out, and you're going to be a sad girl if you think he's going to come home and sit in front of the telly with a tinny, 24 hours a day.

When a bloke gets out of jail after a long stay he runs around like a mad rat, drinking all the piss, eating all the food and pinning tails to every donkey, or should I say ass, he can find.

It doesn't mean you don't love the girl you have at home but it's like boiling water and having nowhere for the steam to go. Then one day the lid gets removed and something's got to blow.'

'It is 5.30am as I write this. I must let my chickens out and feed them and start my general duties on the farm. Paul Manning and I cut several tons of wood the other day and I think we have some other nice jobs lined up for today. It's either dipping sheep, drenching sheep, crutching sheep or shearing fucking sheep or bloody ploughing up the paddocks with the tractor ... And to think I spent years fighting to get out of jail, to do this.'

'Isn't that weird? I have seen men die, seen bodies, poured lime on the cold corpses of drug dealers who deserved to die and then stopped for a mixed grill on the way home, yum.

But the sight of Big Gloria [the hen] dying while she fought for her chicks was too much for the old Chop.'

'As a city boy with simple tastes, I find the bush great fun. I've always been an adaptable fellow and I've quite taken to country life. Chainsawing the guts out of everything is great fun. It's nowhere near as good as turning up the heat on a drug dealer, but it's better than nude Twister.

Trees are in their own way far more dangerous than drug dealers. Put the chainsaw to a drug dealer and they will wriggle and scream and beg and moan. They'll call to God and call their mates on the mobile phone and everything's sweet. But when you give it to a tree at night it can pay you back big time.

One time under moonlight I was giving a big gum the big lash when it paid me back. I had always believed that all things are based on logic. To me it seems perfectly logical to cut a tree down with a chainsaw at night by the light of the moon without being sure which way they may fall. It's sort of Russian Roulette with a giant hardwood.'

'**They reckon you can outrun a tree – after all, it doesn't even have runners, but they keep coming very fast. And in the dark it's luck,**

either good or bad, on which way it falls. As I ran in the dark I knew that if I lived I would always remember the following three lessons ...

Lesson one: never cut a tree down at night;

Lesson two: never cut a tree down at night when you are pissed;

Lesson three: if you do cut a tree down at night when you are pissed, make sure the cool box is in a protected spot.'

'In the old days you'd just wave a chainsaw near a drug dealer and he'd put a grand in your hand just out of good manners. Now as a man of the land I am expected to work like a slave around the sheep shit and flies just to keep the wolf from the door.'

CHOPPER ON ...
EVERYTHING ELSE

'I'd lived with murder contracts over my head for years'

'Don't ask for mercy from a man who has been shown no mercy.'

'Once, when he was young, Dad got the idea that the next-door neighbours were mistreating their family pet. Every time he looked over the fence the animal seemed to be getting thinner and thinner.

He complained to the neighbours, and said he hated cruelty to animals. Every time he asked them if they were feeding the dog, they swore they were. But it seemed skinnier than ever, and one day Dad could take no more. He jumped the fence, threatened the neighbour with a beating, then took the dog and drowned it to put it out of its misery.

It was the first time he had seen a greyhound.'

'If Jesus, the son of God, came down to earth in the 20th century and walked the streets of Melbourne or Sydney, blessing people, healing the sick and turning water into wine, he would be arrested immediately and declared a crackpot.'

'Slip, slop, slap has been my motto. Slip on your shoes, slop some Irish whisky into ya, and slap some lap-dancer on the arse.'

'Keep a mad person confused on a tight rope between anger and kindness and you keep them fascinated.'

'I like the Queen of England and the royal family, although a few of the younger ones could do with a blindfold and a last cigarette. The Queen herself is a lovely old dear.'

'If you're quick on the uptake and able to read between the lines the truth threads its way in and out of every yarn.

It's like the bloke who is writing this book. He has got ears ... you just can't see them.'

'You must remember I was in prison when political correctness crept up on the outside world, which makes me a member of some sort of deprived minority, when you think about it.'

'Sawn-off shotguns, chainsaws, tiger snakes and wives. If you don't take a firm grip they can jump back and bit you.'

'The more I see of people the more I like my dog.'

'The modern prison is a marshmallow compared with good old H. It was the last place from the old hard school and in my heart I preferred the old days to the system that we have now. A good flogging can concentrate the mind.

I did 10 ½ years in 'H', the so-called blood house of the system. It wasn't just my home, I owned the place.

I owned it, I controlled it, I ran it. By ruling that division we ran the jail. We were the most feared gang in the most feared division of the most feared jail in Australia and I was the commanding general.'

'It's like the monkey who roared like a lion at night and made all the animals in the jungle run away in panic and fear.

The monkey started to think he was a lion because all the animals ran in fear of him at night. It was dark, none of the animals could see that the roaring monster was just a little monkey and so the monkey continued to rant and roar.

Even the elephants ran away with the wolves and jackals, and the monkey roared out "I am king of the jungle". Then one night the monkey came across a lion and the monkey roared and growled, but instead of running away in fear the lion charged forward and pounced on the monkey and tore him to shreds.

In the morning all the animals came to look, and when they saw the dead monkey they all cried and asked the lion why he killed the poor monkey. The old lion looked at the dead monkey and, feeling a bit puzzled himself, he said "he's a dead monkey now, but last night he was a lion."

I guess the moral is if you've got a banana in your hand you'd better eat it and stop waving it about trying to pretend it's a shotgun, and if you're a monkey stay in the trees and don't run around the jungle pretending to be a lion. If anybody wants to roar like lions then they better make sure they have the teeth and claws to back it up. I for one have no tears for dead monkeys. The world is full of real dangers, and police are no different from any other people. When you hear the lion roar you either fill it full of lead, or run like a rat. You certainly do not stop to check if it's a real one or you could end up dead. And I'm no police lover, I'm a lover of self defence and I am a great believer in every human having a God-given right to self defence.

I reckon the jungle is becoming too full of monkeys who roar like lions, and when they die all that anyone sees, in hindsight, is the poor dead monkey and they all blame the poor old lion.

I've shot a few of these roaring monkeys myself. Personally I can't stand the little bastards. Mind you, some of them gave me a few "gorillas" if I ever put my hand out. And some were more chumps than chimps.'

'**Here is a story told to me as a small boy by my dear old Dad, who was a sort of a bent Aussie version of Rudyard Kipling or Aesop.**

In relation to the equal division of funds, there is a yarn of the lion, the fox and the donkey who agree to form a partnership and go out hunting. They were the very best of comrades in arms and staunch and solid friends and plundered and killed with scant regard.

At the end of their hunting adventure the lion told the donkey to share the proceeds out. The donkey divided the booty out into three equal parts, making sure to be extra careful and correct that each pile of goodies was exactly the same size and weight.

When he was done the donkey said to the lion, "you are king of the jungle so you have first pick". The lion said "thank you, my dear friend donkey". Then the lion looked at the three large piles of game, gold and goodies and all manner of good things to eat and he turned and sprang at the donkey in a fury and rage and killed and devoured him.

When the lion had finished licking the donkey's blood from his claws, he looked at the terrified fox and said, "Dear old foxy, my fine fellow, would you be so good as to share out and divide the proceeds again in two piles. The donkey, bless his heart, won't be needing his."

The cunning fox then set about collecting all the piles of goodies, gold and game and pushing it into one giant pile leaving only a few small left over tidbits in a very tiny pile for himself. Then the fox said "Lion, my dear fellow, please take your pick."

The lion looked at the tiny pile and then at the

large pile and picked the large pile, then turned and said to the fox, "By the way my dear foxy, who on earth taught you to share things out in such a manner?"

"The donkey," replied the fox. Ha ha.'

'A philospher is someone who points out the bleeding obvious to people who are too thick-headed to think of it themselves.'

'Good blokes are good blokes be they in the bush or in the city and a maggot is a maggot wherever you find him and the bush is no exception.

However, when it's all said and done, where

would I rather live? The bush or the city?
The bush, of course. The snakes are just as
deadly but they move a little slower.'

'A murder today is a tragic horror, but a murder
yesterday is history and all men have a fascination
with history.

'I think my trouble is that I have become a
bit of a sceptical old dinosaur. I've seen too
much and I've become jaded and very
suspicious. The world is changing and I don't
seem to be changing with it ... The whole nation
is turning gay or green in a vomit of political
correctness.'

'I didn't know whether to laugh, cry or shoot.'

'I'm not saying that a legend is nothing but a pack of lies. What I am saying is that one cannot create a legend without the help of a pack of lies. We start with some truth, then add lies to build it up.

Everyone adds another story to the story until we end up with a skyscraper of a legend. The lies are the glue that hold the whole thing together and as a result the lies within each and every legend are the most secret and protected part of the structure.'

'I believe that men should not be allowed to assist in the preparation of any food for health reasons.

Now, men don't like to talk about it, but they all have one thing in common when it comes to the kitchen: they all end up pissing in the sink. There is not a man living who has not at one time or another pissed in the sink.'

'Men are like lino tiles ... lay them the right way once and you can walk over them forever.'

'Basically, it works like this. If I want an extra bit of toast or butter or permission to get a pair of sunglasses sent in, or a gold cross and chain, or a pair of runners or a contact visit, I go to the

Governor of the prison. But anything larger than a contact visit and I have to get down on my knees and call on divine intervention as the Governor is powerless to help. He has the power to punish but his power to grant requests is limited.'

'I have become philosophical about the old hand of fate, particularly when that hand is attached to some arthritic bureaucrat. They are all the same. They are stiffer than a body six hours in the boot. They are given a teaspoonful of power and they want to swing it round like a baseball bat. Oh well, never mind, it's all part of life's rich tapestry.

A rooster one day, feather duster the next.'

'Most of the country people I've met could get work as trick knife tossers in any circus because sticking knives in people's backs is their favourite pastime.'

'It shows me that none of us can ever leave the past. It lies dormant in the back of our skulls and like a dirty big wombat, comes out at night for a sniff around and a scratch.'

'With the entire human race dancing on the edge of it's own grave, who gives a rat's about a few bottom bandits.'

'I received yet another phone call from the movie people wanting me to sign yet another contract.

I've taken a few contracts in my time but nothing like the one the movie people keep running past me.'

'The funny thing about rope is that if you give people enough of it they insist on hanging themselves, and my smiling face and readiness to agree to the most insane arrangements is not politeness; it's rope.'

'The lawyers were paid more than a grand a day. I got a cheese sandwich.'

'In those days Alphonse should have laid off the cake, but what does it matter? Cholesterol didn't kill him, unless the mate who later shot him blew him away with eight cheeseburgers in the back.'

'When a man can admit to himself and others that the world is full of men, twice his size, who could beat him in a fight, then he is well on the way to never being beaten.
I learned that a long time ago.'

'Its easy to separate the real psychos from the false pretenders. Art imitates life and within the criminal world life can also imitate art. It is a stage full of actors. The separation of fact from fiction is almost impossible. Pretenders and role players walk hand in hand with true blue psychopaths.

The difference is that the real psychopath lives in a world all of his own, deep in his own mind. The psycho may very well enjoy the company of actors and role players provided that the psychopath can join in on a drama created by the play actors in a theatre funded by drug dollars.

The psychopath only wants to take part for his own comic reasons no matter if the game is true or false, created by real men of dream merchants. It is of no importance to the psychopath. He doesn't need to rehearse his lines in the play because he is not acting.'

'Let's kill all the lawyers. A wealthy man called his three best friends to his death bed. They were a doctor, a politician and a lawyer. He told each man he wanted to take his money with him when he died. He then gave each man a million dollars and made each man swear to toss the money into his grave after the funeral.

Afterwards, the doctor asked the politician, "Did you toss in all the money?"

"Well, not quite," replied the politician. "I needed half a million for my re-election campaign and a further two hundred thousand for the new medical wing that is being named after me but I did toss in a hundred thousand. I'm sure the good lord and the dear departed will understand."

"Yes," said the doctor. "Speaking of medical

wings, I donated half a million to the medical research unit being named after me and I'm afraid I bought a new car and new house."

"So how much did you toss into the grave?" Asked the politician. The doctor, looking embarrassed, said, "seventy-five thousand."

The lawyer, listening in silence, shook his head in disgust.

"Gentlemen, I'm ashamed of the both of you. I simply cannot believe what I'm hearing," said the lawyer.

The doctor and politician both looked at the lawyer and spoke at once.

"How much did you toss in then?" they asked.

The lawyer held his head up and with a note of pride in his voice said, "Needless to say, gentlemen, I tossed in a cheque for the full amount." It's an old joke but it holds true today.

When a lawyer does you a favour look close, count all your fingers after shaking his hand and kiss your money goodbye. Oh, and don't forget to thank him afterwards. I've sat in a lot of court rooms and I haven't met one lawyer who hasn't tried to talk to me like I'm a mental retard. Criminal lawyers spend most of their time talking to criminals and most criminals are mental retards, therefore the lawyer does develop a superiority complex. It's an occupational hazard, I suppose.'

'Forgiveness and funerals go hand in hand, and the only time to forgive an enemy is after you have seen him die.' – The Jew

'You can talk about slamming someone's knob in a car door, shooting some wombat in the gut, or removing some sucker's toes with a blow torch and that is considered the height of good humour, but mention that someone is a bit on the dusky side and you'll get ten years from the politically correct police.'

'There are some animals in the criminal world who would sell their wife on the streets to buy bullets and teach their kids to steal so Dad can drink the money. Ridding a family of such a man is, to my mind, an act of charity.'

'I had nothing against him personally, but he made his move and lost. In the chess game of life and death, you only get one move.'

'Freddy is a thickset, broad-shouldered, barrel-chested man with the physical strength of a small bull – and the courage of a rice bubble.'

'If the mafia is so tough, why don't they have a branch office in Belfast?'

'What better way to die than to face fearful odds, for the ashes of your family and the honour of your Gods.'

'The psychiatrist and psychologist are God's gift to the mentally ill, proving that God does have a sense of humour.'

'The children of this nation are dying at a faster rate than the bloody trees. Wake up before it is too late.'

'Revenge is a dish best eaten cold, and it has no time limit.'

'If you mix a man with a big mouth and a gangster complex who couldn't punch his way through a lady's lace hanky, you end up with a coward who is eager to impress.'

'Popularity seems to be the pot of gold many people spend their whole lives searching for. I have never bothered to try and look for popularity. Being hated, being unpopular, is safer ground. If you seek popularity, you will generally fail, ending up a pathetic figure of scorn and ridicule. You can even destroy yourself in the process. But men who are hated can actually gain a following of loyal admirers, while some who seek popularity end up being disliked and hated. These are people who won't stand up for what they believe in, but act only to be liked by others. People end up seeing through them.

It is a confusing psychological topic. It is strange because I have received mail from people who reckon I'm great, because I'm the biggest arsehole they have ever heard of. So you figure it out.'

'There are other prison officers here who like to think they are heavy thinkers. One of them loves to sit down with me and have huge psychological debates about the pros and cons of the human mind. He has locked me into some debates which have left me in dire need of a Panadol and a good lie down.

He likes to climb inside your head and pick, pick, pick at your brain. My method is more likely to creep up behind you and go whack, whack, whack with an ice-pick.'

'If bastards and bad men are so hated, why do good men love to read about them?'

'We are all in search of the Holy Grail, the ultimate truth, the meaning of life. If God came down to earth and we all sat at his feet and asked, "Lord, tell us the answer," he would say, "Piss off, I'm trying to find where I came from."'

'The guy was a mental peanut with the physical courage of dishwater.'

'This personal stupid, blind courage of honest men outweighs the personal courage of bad men. Why? Because bad men hold very little dear to their heart, whereas the honest man will often risk life and limb fighting with an intruder over a bloody television set or video.'

'I've got enough heavy duty firepower and ammo stored away to hold off a small army for three months. I believe that when Australia is invaded, those who are not prepared will die ... but the buggers won't get me without a fight.'

'Instead of ranting and raving, rolling about and sooking at the injustice of it all, I simply look at it this way: it is never checkmate until I'm dead; until then, it is just another move on the board.

They make their move, I make mine. I don't take it personally and I hope they don't either.

By getting angry I would lose my edge. Wars are won by men who are willing to fight them for a long time.'

'And I am a man with a long, long memory. Shallow people and false pretenders don't have long memories. They will forget, but I won't. I don't have to shoot people to punish them. There are more easy ways to kill a cat than by wringing its neck. The cats in question used up their nine lives when they betrayed my trust and friendship, let me tell you.'

'**On my daily walks to the prison hospital from the remand yard to get my vitamin tablet I found, much to my delight, seven big, fat snails, bloody big buggers. Anyone who has been to jail knows that all prisoners become first class scroungers and learn that anything they can find to use they will grab with both hands.**

Now the sight of seven snails was too great a temptation to me. I scooped the blighters up and asked one of the screws to boil up some water for me. I placed the snails in the water and let them soak for about 10 minutes. I then got some more boiling water and gave them another 10 minutes. That seemed to slow them down, in a manner of speaking. They were easy then to pop out of their shells.

I got hold of some silver paper, some salt, pepper, garlic powder and a spoonful of butter. I didn't have a French cookbook so I had to do the best I could. In prison, nouvelle Cuisine is anything cooked by a first-year apprentice cook. I got the recently deceased snails, minus their shells, and wrapped them in the silver paper, with the salt, pepper, butter and garlic powder. I placed the lot on the grill under the big toaster in the remand yard dining room …

… I felt I was getting the hang of the French cooking. In fact, with my experience with meat cleavers I thought that when I got out of jail I would go into the culinary business.

I was confident, perhaps too confident, about my cooking skills. The little buggers finally had their revenge. I had plenty of time to think about my mistakes as I was sitting on the toilet. I know about severe stomach pains, having been stabbed in the guts once or twice, and let me tell you, the snails were tougher than a steak knife attack.

I was shivering and shaking and thought I was at death's door. I have suffered bad cases of Bombay Bottom, at the hands of Mad Dog's curried veggies in Pentridge and Slim Minogue's chilli powder delights, but that pales into nothing compared with the revenge of the killer snails.

It was then I learned a very important lesson about cooking the more exotic dishes. If one insists on eating garlic snails, one should always know that the snails themselves have not gobbled a gutful of snail bait. The little green pellets turned out to be snail poison and the buggers I had been eating were the gung-ho survivors of more chemicals than Chernobyl.'